THE DEAN'S INTRODUCTION

Lincoln Cathedral is one of the greatest, yet one of the least known, medieval buildings of Europe. Perched high on its hill overlooking the ancient city and dominating the skyline for many miles, it has a visual impact which is nothing less than startling. At the peak of its development it was, after all, some twenty metres taller than the Great Pyramid.

Built mainly between 1072 and 1280 with additions and alterations right up to this century, it manages, despite its fascinating stylistic variety, to give a striking sense of purposeful unity. It is fortunate in having few tombs or monuments to mar that first and continuing impression of vast, echoing space with glorious colour from the windows enhancing the dignity and splendour of the soaring pillars of local limestone and Purbeck marble.

But the Cathedral is more than an architectural marvel; even the clutter of scaffolding, so irritating to the visitor (and especially the photographer), demonstrates the level of the maintenance and care it is receiving as the battle against decay and pollution continues. For here is not only a building but a complex and vigorous community committed to the worship of God – a living church. At the very centre of that community lies a regular round of sung services in the great tradition of English choral music. To these as to almost all our other activities the visitor is most heartily welcome.

The Dean and Chapter – those priests who are responsible for this great church – see it as a place of meeting between person and person as well as between people and God. All who work here, whether in our shops and offices, school and choirs, as masons, plumbers, joiners and mechanics, priests, monks and nuns, musicians, vergers and bell ringers, flower arrangers, volunteers and regular staff, work to one end – that God be praised, and in that praising, our guests, the tourists, discover more of the splendour of God's creation.

'A View of Lincoln Cathedral from the West, 1742' by Joseph Baker (d.1770). Opposite: the Nave looking west

THE BUILDING OF THE CATHEDRAL

A Cathedral is a church containing the Bishop's seat, or *cathedra*. William the Conqueror's decision in 1072 to transfer the see or base of the Bishop of this diocese from the quiet backwater of Dorchester-on-Thames to the busy fortified city of Lincoln was a masterstroke. Remigius of Fécamp (Bishop 1067-1092) had assisted William at the invasion and was the first Norman to be made a Bishop after the Conquest. Remigius was given land for a new cathedral church to replace the existing mother church of this area, St. Mary's, which was served by the clergy who lived as a community but who worked in the district round the city. The word 'Minster' describes this kind of church and has survived.

The Norman cathedral built between 1072 and 1092 was impressive and fortress-like. An account written in the mid-12th century describes it as 'Strong as the place was strong and fair as the place was fair. Dedicated to the Virgin of virgins, it was to be pleasing to God and, as was needed at the time, unconquerable by enemies'. Sadly Remigius died days before the consecration. A fire severely damaged the roof of the building in 1141 and the third bishop, Alexander the Magnificent (1123-48), is credited with much restoration work. This included replacing the wooden ceiling with stone vaults, and the decoration of the West Front, including the three doorways in the recesses. The remarkable Romanesque frieze was inserted above the west doorways and is at present undergoing extensive and detailed restoration.

This great church was largely destroyed by earthquake in April 1185. Only the West Front and lower stages of the western towers survive to testify to the splendour of the first cathedral. Under the inspired leadership of Bishop Hugh (1186-1200) work began on rebuilding in 1192 (see pp. 14 and 30).

A WALK AROUND THE CATHEDRAL

THE CENTRAL DOORWAY

Despite restoration this Norman doorway is magnificent in size and decoration. The figures of hunters, animals and birds intertwined in foliage on the columns lead the eye up to the delicately carved capitals, and the arch with its rich mixture of chevron, rosettes and beakhead ornament. Fierce dragon heads terminate the hood over the arch. The gallery of kings, inserted in the 14th Century, possibly represents the Kings of England from William I to Edward III.

THE NAVE

The word is derived from the Latin for 'ship' and, like an up-turned hull, this noble space is used for great public occasions, such as the enthronement of a new Bishop, services of commemoration, concerts and exhibitions.

The nave was built during the first half of the 13th century in the style known as Early English Gothic, based on the pointed arch. The clustered piers of Purbeck marble and local limestone with their stiff-leaf capitals support a triforium and a clerestory which lights one of the earliest vaults in England to use intermediate ribs, or tiercerons. The great bosses, or keystones, which mark the intersections of these ribs are carved with Gothic foliage which is found in profusion in the Cathedral. The fine proportions of the nave give it an appearance of lightness remarkable for a space of this size. Originally, the marble shone, the floor would have been covered in dark tomb slabs filled with brass figures and inscriptions, and the stonework would have been bright with paint, vestiges of which can be seen, restored, in the decorations marking some of the vaulting ribs in the nave and its aisles. The names on the vault probably indicate 13th century benefactors; certainly a William Paris was Mayor of Lincoln in the 1240s when the nave was built.

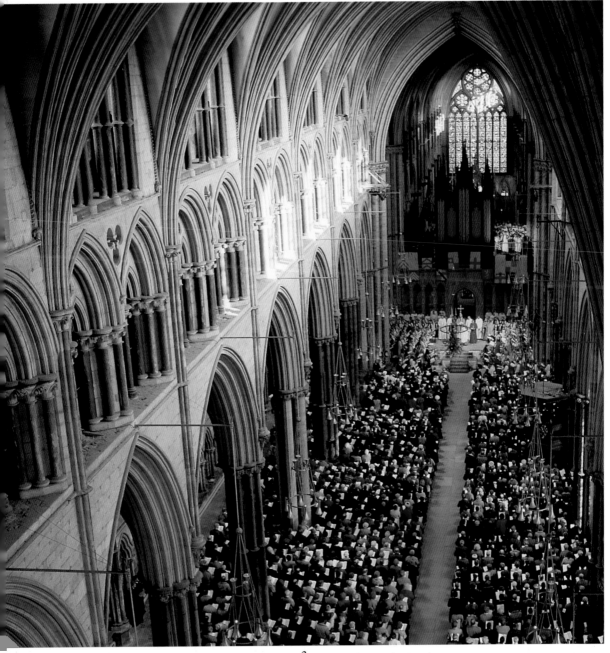

THE MORNING CHAPEL

This chapel, also known as the St. Mary Magdalene Chapel, was used in the 13th Century as a parish church until Bishop Sutton (1280-1299) had a new church built where the present St. Mary Magdalene's stands beside the Exchequer-gate. The central vault springs from a delicate and graceful Purbeck marble shaft. The altar frontal was designed and made by Constance Howard in 1966 and shows the jar of ointment, the tears and hair of Mary Magdalene, with which she washed and anointed Christ's feet. The image of the hair is continued in the design of the hassocks, made by the Lincolnshire Embroiderers' Guild. A temporary display at the rear contains magnificent examples of Romanesque sculpture. Close to the Morning Chapel is the memorial to Bishop Kaye.

Bishop Kaye's Memorial

The peaceful figure of the Bishop (1827-1853) lying Bible in hand as if asleep does not seem likely to have caused a stir, but when it first appeared those who had subscribed to the sculpture were offended – the pose was altogether too casual for them. The monument is in Carrara marble – designed by G. F. Bodley and executed by Richard Westmacott junior in 1857. The Bishop, who had been a notable scholar, was buried at Riseholme, just outside Lincoln, where the Bishops of Lincoln had their home 1837-1885.

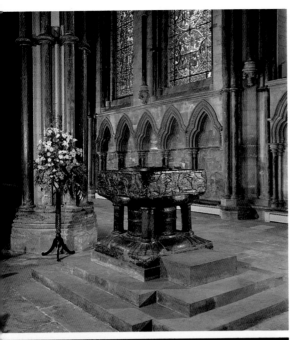

The Font

This fine, rare example of Tournai work from Flanders has been dated to the mid 12th Century, and so survived the earthquake of 1185. The very dark stone is limestone marble quarried from the banks of the river Escaut, near Tournai. Mythical dragons and griffins, medieval symbols of evil and vigilance, circle the font, which is still used for baptisms, though the deep lead-lined basin is no longer filled. Those who know Winchester Cathedral's font will recognise the same style and material. The more modern steps, placed there in 1890, are of Ashford Black Limestone from Derbyshire.

The Nave Glass

The stained glass windows in the Nave are of the mid 19th Century. They imitate windows of the 13th Century and on the south side show scenes from the Old Testament, on the north all but one panel from the New Testament. The cinquefoil window of the 13th Century and the 14th Century window below it at the West End are also filled with glass of the mid 19th Century. That in the Great West Window by the Sutton brothers (1862) shows ten Old Testament kings and incorporates some fragments of medieval glass.

The Romanesque Tombstone (A)

This rare Tournai marble slab was once associated with the first bishop, Remigius, but its style and material make it more likely to be that of the third bishop, Alexander (1123-48), who did so much to beautify the Cathedral in the mid 12th Century. It shows a Jesse tree, the genealogical tree of Christ, with David, the son of Jesse, the enthroned Virgin and Christ seated and flanked by tiny angels and other figures. The damage to it may have been caused by the earthquake of 1185, or an earlier fire.

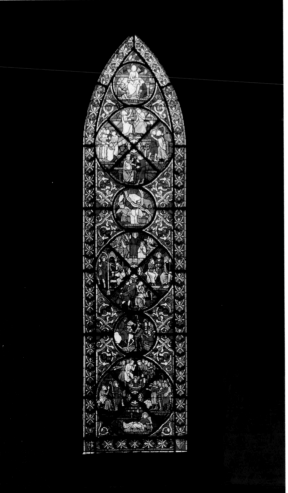

Left: the Joseph Window in the South Nave Aisle (c. 1860)

THE GREAT TRANSEPT

The Nave leads into the Crossing; here the space known as the Great Transept is lit by two wonderful circular, or rose, windows with lancets below each. As early as the 1220s a biography of St. Hugh describes these two windows as the 'Two eyes of the Cathedral'. The Dean's Eye faced north

'protecting against the Devil of cold and darkness,' while the Bishop's looked south 'to receive the Holy Spirit.' With the glass in the East End Aisle windows of the Cathedral, these windows make up the third most important collection of medieval glass in an English cathedral after Canterbury and York.

The Screen or Pulpitum

This magnificent stone screen of the early 14th Century, used then as a pulpit, marks the division between the main public and liturgical spaces. It was once even more eye catching, for the stone work was painted in brilliant colour, traces of which can still be seen. A closer look reveals a gallery of little figures, animals, saints, acrobats and grotesques, which remind us that to the carvers all creation seen or imagined was equally valid for inclusion in the decoration. This is the Decorated style in full glory.

The Organ

There has been an organ of some kind in the Cathedral from as far back as the 14th Century. On a desk front c. 1370 in St. Hugh's Choir an angel can be seen playing a portable organ which was held on the lap, or set on a table. Accounts of 1311 and 1442 mention fees for cleaning or setting up a new organ. The present organ with its Gothic case, designed by E. W. Willson, was first erected on the screen in 1826 and enlarged and improved in subsequent alterations, most notably by 'Father' Henry Willis in 1898. The organ was given a complete restoration and a new console in 1960 by the Durham firm of Harrison & Harrison Limited. William Byrd is the best known of the Cathedral's organists; he was about 20 when appointed in 1563, and went from here to the Chapel Royal, London, in 1572.

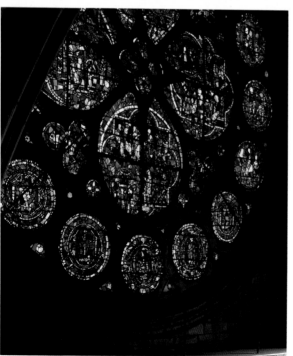

The Dean's Eye

The Dean's Eye is the only rose window in England of this date, the early 13th Century, which still contains a considerable quantity of its original glass. The main theme of the window is that of the Last Judgment, but there are scenes showing incidents from the Legend of the Life of the Virgin Mary, and the funeral of St. Hugh, who died in 1200. Christ in Majesty sits in the heart of the window in gold and red, his arm raised. The plate tracery places the window as early as 1210. The glass was last restored in 1855 and at present it is very fragile. The painted glass in the five lancets below, 'Grisaille' glass, offered a more restrained quality of light; similar glass is found alongside coloured glass of the period, notably in York Minster.

The Bishop's Eye

The Bishop's Eye departs from the early medieval concept of a rose window containing Christ or the Virgin Mary at its heart. It is a replacement of an earlier rose and was inserted about 1330 when the gable end was rebuilt. Recent research

Above: the Dean's Eye in the north limb of the Great Transept
Left: a detail of the Dean's Eye window. Opposite: the screen and organ – choristers and their master enter St. Hugh's Choir

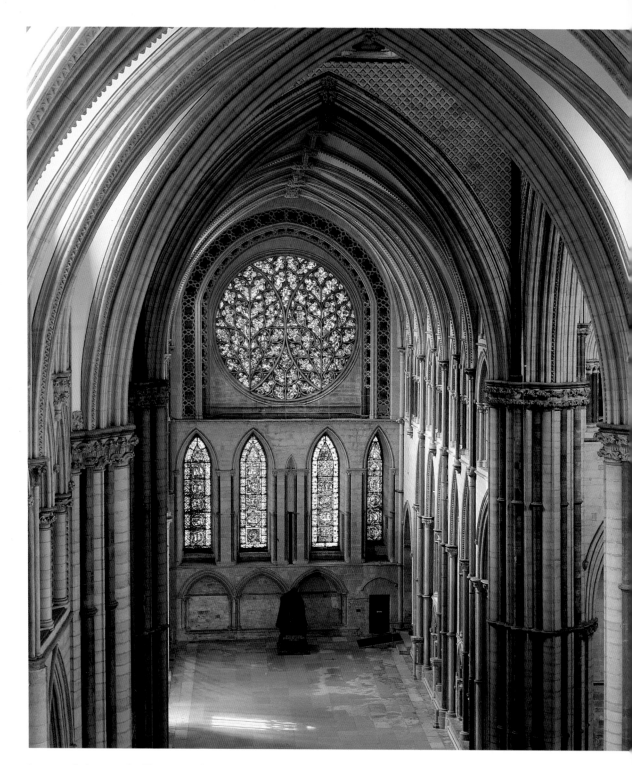

has revealed some significant remains of the original 14th Century glass which, as in the Dean's Eye, appears to show scenes from the Last Judgment. The glowing fragments of medieval glass reset in the late 18th Century, the flowing leaf-tracery of the window and the superb open stonework of the frame makes this one of the most impressive and unusual windows anywhere in Europe.

Below it, in the lancets, are medallions of 13th Century glass, not in their original position but probably reset also in the 18th Century. Scenes from the Legend of St. Nicholas can be seen in the second lancet from the left, while the lowest medallion in the second lancet from the right shows the appealing scene of King David feigning madness, dancing on his hands and wearing red stockings.

Memorial to Dean Honywood (1660-82) (C³)

Dean Honywood had the heavy task of restoring the fabric and music after the Civil War, and had to re-assert the rights and privileges of Chapter which had lapsed during the Cromwellian period. During his exile in the Netherlands he had purchased a great number of books and these he willed to the Dean and Chapter, along with the Library which he got Wren to design and for which he paid. His memorial describes him as 'a man of munificence and liberality whose abiding memorial is the Library which he enriched with books not few in number and of no ordinary kind'; he made bequests to all members of the Cathedral body, including vergers, ringers and sweepers.

The Monument of Bishop Edward King (1885-1910) (C¹)

A great pastoral bishop, much loved in the diocese and with a saintly reputation, Bishop King was involved in disputes about the amount of ritual used in parish churches of his diocese. His trial to answer charges of high church practices was an unhappy event, but his acquittal marked the end of attempts at state regulation of ritual. He is buried in the Cloister Garth. The statue in bronze (1913) is by W. B.

Richmond, with lettering by Eric Gill. It shows the Bishop in the act of confirmation, and was intended to stand in the open.

Memorial to Dean Fuller (1635-1700) (C²)

Samuel Fuller held the office of Dean of Lincoln from 1695 to his death in 1700. He was ordained by his uncle Archbishop Thomas Fuller and became Chancellor of Lincoln and Chaplain to the King. The mural and ceiling painter Antonio Verrio used his face as the model for 'Bacchus astride of a barrel'. Looking at the monument it is easy to understand why.

Above: wall plaque to Dean Honywood in the Nave

Left: Bishop Edward King's dramatic monument in the South Transept

Right: wall monument to Dean Fuller in the South Transept

Opposite: the Bishop's Eye window in the North Transept

THE SERVICES' CHAPELS

These three former Chantry Chapels are in the Great North Transept. The concept of a Services' Chapel in memory of the dead of the First World War grew from the dedication of the first of them, to St. George, as the Regimental Chapel of the Lincolnshire Regiment in 1914. In 1923 the Chapels of St. Michael and St. Andrew were restored and re-dedicated to airmen and seamen respectively and all three were re-decorated and dedicated in 1946 as a Services' Memorial Chapel – a thank offering for peace after the Second World War.

The Soldiers' Chapel (8) contains the Books of Memory of the 10th Foot which became the Lincolnshire Regiment and finally the 2nd Battalion, The Royal Anglian Regiment. The oldest colour dates from 1685. The glass in this chapel is by Archibald Nicholson (1926), with the themes of Sacrifice and Victory.

The Seamen's Chapel (7) has glass by Christopher Webb (1956) showing famous early Lincolnshire settlers and explorers of the United States and Australia, among them Captain John Smith, George Bass, Matthew Flinders and Sir Joseph Banks, also Bishop J. C. Patterson the saintly first Bishop of Melanesia. Some of the fragile ensigns are topped by crowns showing that a sovereign presented them. The model is of H.M.S. Investigator, in which Matthew Flinders charted the coast of Australia.

The Airmen's Chapel (6) contains four impressive stained glass windows made between 1953 and 1966 by Harry Stammers of York. The four archangels, Saints Gabriel, Michael and Raphael, with Uriel, are shown each with their symbolic attributes as interveners in the life and death of man. Here also are overseas memorials, the Books of Remembrance of Groups 1 and 5 Bomber Command, and 9 Training Command, with over twenty-five thousand names.

The Airmen's Chapel altar. Because of the strong links with airmen who flew locally in the last war, communion is celebrated here weekly by an RAF Chaplain. Opposite: the Services' Chapels

THE CHOIR AISLES

The 13th Century carved doorways (D) leading from the Crossing into the Choir Aisles are masterpieces of the stone carvers' art. Round each arch runs a band of open-work foliage, while between Purbeck marble shafts either side of each doorway there are bands of roses and dogtooth decoration. The finely carved capitals are only just above eye level.

The double arcading along the outer walls of the choir aisles is unusual and visually intriguing. Against the wall are arches in relief with a second layer in front of them giving the illusion of a passage way along the wall. From the spandrels, or spaces between the arches, busts of angels and other figures peer out. The capitals are varied and boldly carved with stylised leaves. The aisle floors contain the remains of memorials formerly in the Nave. The brass was removed by Parliamentarian soldiers in May 1644.

Opposite: doorway to South Choir Aisle

Right: detail of South Choir Aisle screen showing a bird carrying a worm to her fledglings and flying off again

Below left: mid-15th century south German woodcarving showing Christ and St. Veronica

Below right: empty matrices of long destroyed brasses in the aisle floor

Built in the first phase of the second Cathedral (1192-1200), these Transepts are full of architectural interest, showing teasing inconsistencies in structure and work of assured skill in the decoration. The small rounded chapels in the French style were part of Bishop Hugh's scheme for his choir's eastern end. One of the most intriguing features is the *Trondheim Pillar* (L) at the inner western corner of each transept. Three boldly crocketed limestone shafts embraced by Purbeck shafts rising to stiff leaf capitals form a cluster of striking impact; even the Purbeck shafts are alternating rounded and fluted. Trondheim, or Nidaros, Cathedral has similar 'Lincoln Pillars' as its eastern end, showing that there was a movement of masons from Lincoln to Norway in the late 12th Century. See page 26.

Bishop Grosseteste's Tomb (16)

Robert Grosseteste was one of the most famous of Lincoln's medieval bishops (1235-1253). A distinguished scholar, theologian and proto-scientist, he was involved in the development of Oxford University from his time as a student, and was later its first Chancellor. He was energetic and fearless, a supporter of the growing Franciscan Order in England, and a strong disciplinarian in his diocese. The Nave was completed in his time and other work associated with his name is the diaper work on some inner and outer sections of the West Front, and also on the lower inner stage of the Central Tower which collapsed c.1237 and had to be rebuilt.

Robert Grosseteste was venerated as a saint after his death, but he had been too outspoken against Rome to be canonised. His splendid tomb on the site of this memorial was destroyed in the Civil War. The present tomb was designed by Randall Blacking and re-dedicated in July 1953. Lincoln Training College was re-named Bishop Grosseteste College at its centenary in 1962.

Left: Grosseteste's modern tomb executed by John Skelton, stands outside the Chapel of St. Peter and St. Paul, now associated with education

Opposite: the South East Transept showing part of Bishop Grosseteste's tomb

ST. HUGH

Henry II's choice of *Hugh of Avalon* to be Bishop of Lincoln (1186-1200) the year after the earthquake of 1185 came at a crucial moment in the Cathedral's history, and there is a sense in which the entire second cathedral owes its being to him. Hugh was a monk of the austere Carthusian order from whose headquarters, the Grande Chartreuse, he had been summoned c. 1179 by Henry II in order to take charge of a small Carthusian priory at Witham in Somerset, endowed as part of Henry's penance for Archbishop Thomas à Becket's murder. Hugh's reluctance to become bishop of the largest diocese in England was not surprising; he returned each summer to Witham to re-enter the strict monastic life for a while. Hugh spent six years in preparation, gathering funds, architect and craftsmen to start the re-building of the Cathedral, and his biographers describe the profound effect

Hugh's leadership had on the task. His consecration heralded a century of change and development in the city and diocese as a great new Gothic building rose from the largely cleared site of the Norman cathedral. He brought famous teachers to be members of the Lincoln Chapter. Hugh died in 1200, his reputation as a saint already drawing pilgrims to the incomplete cathedral; only its eastern transepts and Choir were finished by his death.

In 1220 the Pope declared Hugh a saint and ordered his body to be transferred to a worthier place (see p.20). There were delays in carrying out the order as work on completing the Gothic nave westwards continued. By the mid-13th Century St. Hugh's cathedral was complete, and the remains of the Norman west end had been incorporated into the Gothic work of the great screen front.

ST. HUGH'S CHOIR

This is the heart of the Cathedral. The iron scroll-work screens and gates which date from the late 13th Century effectively link the sanctuary with the choir to form an inner church where the Liturgy, or worship, continues daily.

The character and atmosphere of St. Hugh's Choir is largely created by the impressive oak stalls with their complex and delicate carpentry – one of the finest sets in England. Each medieval stall has its own pinnacled taber-nacle with a saint from the Anglican calendar inserted above each in the 1890s. Five later stalls on the north side have Queen Victoria and four English Kings in the niches. The stalls date from c. 1370 and each has its own intriguing carved tip-up seat, or misericord. The name of John of Welbourn (died 1380), is associated with the stalls in his capacity as Treasurer of the cathedral at the time they were made. Above each stall the canon's medieval prebendum, or source of income is found, together with the first line of the

Carved misericord in St. Hugh's Choir

psalm allotted to that stall. Each canon had his stall in the upper range, and below it the stall of his vicar, or substitute. Present-day canons – the statutes provide for fifty-three – have few obligations and the medieval prebends are no longer sources of income, but the division of the Psalter among the canons means that each canon is still bidden at his installation to say his Psalm every day 'if nothing hinders'.

The architecture here is Early English, characterised by the pointed arch, liberal use of Purbeck or Alwalton (Peter-borough) marble shafts, lancet windows, finely carved capitals, and ribbed vault. This vault, sometimes called the 'crazy vault', is unique in England for its asymmetrical scissor-like patterning. Comparison with the vault of the Angel Choir will give a clear impression of the ingenuity of the architect. Arguments continue as to the merits or de-merits of this vault. The roof timbers have been dated c.1200.

Angel with early hurdy-gurdy

THE SANCTUARY (H)

Beyond the step and brass rail the celebration of the Holy Communion or Eucharist reaches its climax on Sunday mornings. The priest consecrates bread and wine at the altar and, assisted by other clergy, administers them to the members of the congregation who come to kneel at the rail. Everything here is concentrated on heightening people's consciousness of the holy – the altar frontal and the vestments, suitably coloured for the particular period of the church's year, the plate, candles and flowers.

The Sanctuary stone-work is deceptive. The six bays on the north which appear to be two tombs are work of about 1300; the Swynford Chantry opposite them is early 15th Century; the rest of the enclosure was designed by the architect and restorer, James Essex, in 1769. The three-gabled reredos or altar framework, is influenced by the monument of Bishop de Luda at Ely, that is, in the style of about 1300, which links it sensitively with the style of the Angel Choir and Easter Sepulchre. The central arch above the altar was once filled with the painting of the Annunciation by the Reverend William Peters, done in 1798 and now on the North East Transept wall.

The Easter Sepulchre

Like the Judgment Porch, this tomb of Christ is the only one of its kind to be found in an English Cathedral, and dates to c.1300. The figures of three sleeping soldiers guard the tomb, each leaning on his shield and dressed in chain mail. To the west, the tomb of Remigius who, after his death, was venerated locally as a saint, enjoys the closest proximity to the sepulchre.

The tomb of Remigius and the Easter Sepulchre

Katherine Swynford's Chantry

Katherine Swynford's tomb has a special appeal for visitors. She was married young to a Lincolnshire knight, Hugh Swynford. After his death she remained a widow for many years until her marriage in the Cathedral in January 1396 to John of Gaunt, Duke of Lancaster and Earl of Lincoln, made her one of the most important women in the land. The four

Katherine Swynford's chantry

children of her long previous association with the Duke were surnamed Beaufort and retrospectively legitimised by both the Pope and Richard II soon after the marriage. Despite the proviso by their half brother, Henry IV (born at Bolingbroke Lincolnshire), that no Beaufort should succeed to the throne, Queen Elizabeth II is descended through Henry VII's mother, Lady Margaret Beaufort, from John Earl of Somerset, the eldest Beaufort son. Katherine lived for a period in the present Chancery on the east side of Minster Yard. Her sister was the wife of Geoffrey Chaucer. This memorial chapel for Katherine, who died in 1403, and her daughter, Joan Beaufort, later Countess of Westmorland was raised in the early 15th Century. It has a prominent place in the Sanctuary close to the high altar. Though the tombs have been re-arranged and stripped of their brasses, the chantry, with its fine carving of the screen-work and capitals and the remarkable canopy covered in net tracery, is a fitting memorial to a distinguished and beautiful woman.

THE ANGEL CHOIR

Bishop Hugh was made a saint in 1220, a process which involved the presentation of evidence concerning miracles performed by him before, during and after his death. Pope Honorius III sent instructions, with the Bull of Canonization, for the Saint's body to have a suitably worthy memorial. The St. John Baptist Chapel in the N.E. Transept

The visceral tomb of Queen Eleanor. Opposite: the Angel Choir

which contained Hugh's tomb was enlarged for this purpose. As the cult of St. Hugh grew, a bold scheme took shape to place a new shrine as the focus of the whole Cathedral. Work began in 1256 on the building of the Angel Choir. With its noble proportions, outstanding stonework and sculpture and great east wall of light it replaced the 'chevet' ending of Hugh's church with its more restricted spaces. The black lines on the floor indicate the former east walls.

The new choir was ready for the translation of St. Hugh's body on October 6th, 1280, when in the presence of Edward I and Queen Eleanor, and a great ecclesiastical and aristocratic gathering, Hugh's body was exhumed for transferring to the prepared shrine. The head became detached from the body and received its own shrine, the remains of which lie below the East Window and are still honoured. Sadly, the body shrine which was elevated above the old reredos and which was a marvel of richness before 1540, has gone altogether.

The East Window, the earliest and largest eight-light window in England, measures 59 ft. x 30 ft. and is a superb example of bar tracery, filled now with its third glass, from 1855, designed by Charles Winston and made by Ward and Hughes. The medallions make a cross of scenes showing the life, death and Resurrection of Christ and some of the miracles.

St. Hugh's Head Shrine (19)

Lincoln ranked as the third greatest pilgrimage centre in England. Prayers at the shrines were the high point of any pilgrimage. Henry VIII ordered the Head Shrine to be stripped of its jewels in 1539 and just over a century later, during the Civil War, the head and its reliquary disappeared: fortunately a drawing of the Shrine was made in 1641, shortly before the theft. The adornment, designed by David Poston, the sculptor and jeweller, was set here in 1986 to mark the 800th anniversary of Bishop Hugh's arrival in Lincoln. It is made of stainless steel covered in bronze.

Eleanor of Castile's Visceral Tomb (20)

Isolated below the great East Window is the tomb of Eleanor of Castile, Queen to Edward I. She died at Harby, Nottinghamshire, only a few miles from Lincoln, in November 1290, and her remains were buried in three different holy places; her body in Westminster Abbey, her heart in London's Blackfriars, and her viscera or internal organs in Lincoln. The marriage to Edward lasted 35 years and she bore him at least 13 children, some on her journeys with him, even on Crusade. The twelve Eleanor Crosses erected by Edward after her death to mark the resting places of the funeral cortege on its way to Westminster were famous landmarks of which only three survive. The tomb was destroyed by Parliamentarian soldiers. Fortunately, a drawing of it had been made in 1641 so that when Mr. Joseph Ruston of Lincoln paid for its restoration in 1890 a copy was possible, with the bronze figure the replica of that by William Torel on Eleanor's tomb in Westminster Abbey. The shields on the plinth bear the arms of Leon, Castile, England and Ponthieu, and there are small lions and castles on the pillows under Eleanor's head.

Left: the famous Lincoln Imp. Opposite: St. Hugh's Head Shrine

The Imp (above 19)

The Imp probably owes its fame to being in such close proximity to St. Hugh's Head Shrine. Pilgrims would easily have spotted the brightly painted grotesque, looked down on by the painted angels (below the upper windows) who proverbially turned him to stone for misbehaving. More recently, the Imp became widely known as a good luck symbol after King Edward VII, when Prince of Wales, had been presented with a gold imp scarf pin, which he is reputed to have worn in 1896 when his horse 'Persimmon' won the Derby.

Other Tombs and Shrines

Round the walls on the floor of the Retro-Choir, the area behind the High Altar, there are several interesting tombs and memorials. Close together are the 15th Century tomb of Bishop Fleming (22) (1420-31) with its Chantry Chapel behind it, and the Memorial to St. Gilbert of Sempringham.

Bishop Fleming was the founder of Lincoln College Oxford and the association with Lincoln College continues to this day, the present Bishop being its Visitor. The tomb is an early example of a cadaver tomb – it was intended to remind people that however great they were in this world after death they would all be alike.

Left: the Fleming Chantry and St. Gilbert memorial
Below: the Russell Chantry with murals by Duncan Grant (1885-1978) showing scenes connected with the wool trade as the Chapel is dedicated to St. Blaise, patron saint of woolcombers
Opposite: another view of the Angel Choir

The great candle-holders and pots in memory of Gilbert of Sempringham in this diocese (1083-1189) were designed by Robin Welch in 1984 and commemorate the 12th Century saint and the Order he founded, the only English religious order, the Gilbertines. The tall pots represent the men of the Order, the plumper ones the women, while the stumpy pot stands for Gilbert who was known to be deformed. As a very old man, Gilbert would have met Bishop Hugh soon after his arrival in Lincoln, so this 20th Century memorial is fittingly placed next to the remains of St. Hugh's Head Shrine.

Other near-by tombs include those of the distinguished 14th Century Burghersh family in their chantry of St. Catherine, with its fine 13th Century glass, recently restored. Close by the Fleming Chantry is the tomb slab commemorating Robert Dymoke d. 1735, an ancestor of the present Queen's Champion, an hereditary title belonging to this Lincolnshire family. The elaborate monument next to it is to Bishop Christopher Wordsworth (1869-1885), a noted hymn-writer and the poet's nephew. He set up many of the Diocese's church schools and founded Lincoln Theological College.

NORTH EAST TRANSEPT

The Treasury (T), designed by Louis Oman with glass by Geoffrey Clarke, was established in 1960 by the Goldsmiths' Company and contains fine silver plate from Diocesan churches and personal plate of the Cathedral's medieval bishops. There is fine wrought iron scroll work on the original medieval door to this Chapel, which was known as the Medicine Chapel. The painting above the door is of four 12th Century bishops of Lincoln, and was commissioned from the Venetian painter Damini in c. 1727, probably as a restoration, since there is evidence of medieval paint beneath. There are support beams embedded in the wall

structure of this chapel, similar to those more striking beams which stretch between St. Hugh's Choir and the Angel Choir at a point of stress.

The Chapel next to the Cloister door is most probably the Chapel of St. John the Baptist, in which St. Hugh's body lay in state in the years from his death in 1200 until the translation to the Angel Choir Shrine in 1280. Evidence dates the extension to this Chapel (now marked out in the grass to the East) to c. 1225 and this would coincide with the date of the canonization, and the need for greater space for pilgrims as the *cultus* grew.

THE CLOISTER

Built at the very end of the 13th century, the Cloister provided a covered walk between the Cathedral and the Chapter House. Strictly speaking, the Cloister was an extravagance, for the Cathedral was not a monastic foundation. The particular appeal of this Cloister lies in its oak vault and bosses which, like the bosses in the rest of the Cathedral, were once painted and gilded. There are some remarkable sculptures here which include religious subjects, such as the Virgin and Child, animals, foliage and hybrid creatures. The Cloister has been used as a burial place from a date soon after its erection: on the wall of the south walk is the tombstone of Richard of Gainsborough, possibly the master mason involved in the building of the Angel Choir; his death date being 1300 or later.

Opposite: the Trondheim Pillar at the corner of the North Transept and North Aisle. Right: one of 62 bosses in the Cloister dating from c.1299. It has fine detail in the eyes and mouth(M)

THE CHAPTER HOUSE

This beautiful building, dating from the mid-13th Century, is built polygonally round a central pillar with fluted Purbeck shafts. Above the arcaded walls are lancets with 19th Century glass containing the main events in the Cathedral's history up to the visit of John Wesley in 1797. The Chapter House is the secular meeting place of the Cathedral. It is used nowadays for a variety of social and artistic events, but in the past it has witnessed many splendid or disturbing occasions.

Edward I called one of the very first English Parliaments here in 1301 at which he declared his son, Edward o Caernafon, the first Prince of Wales. The suppression of the Knights Templars was speeded by the trial held in the Chapter House in 1310, and in October 1536 the leaders o the Lincolnshire Rising gathered here to receive King Henr VIII's reply to their demands. Today, the yearly gatherings o the Canons for the Greater Chapter Meeting or the inductio of a new Canon are reminders of the building's origina function as a Council Chamber for the Capitulum, the Chapter or governing body of the Cathedral.

THE WREN LIBRARY

From the Cloister, the Library can be seen as a gallery over a classical arcade of nine arches which, at the time of its construction, replaced the ruined north walk of the Cloister. Christopher Wren designed the Library for Dean Honywood's personal collection of books, and it was built in 1674-5 at a cost to the Dean of £780. A doorway at the west end was originally Honywood's private entrance from the former Deanery, now demolished. The Library is a long, narrow, elegant apartment with shelving along the north side. It has recently been completely and magnificently restored to its original colour scheme, as envisaged by Wren, with grey and white marbled panels between the window on the south side and at the west end. Around the mai doorway at the east end, five layers of paint have been pains takingly scraped away to reveal the original delicate decoration

The Cathedral has had a collection of books since the 12t Century, and the earliest surviving Library in the building now known as the Medieval Library – was built betwee 1420 and 1422. This Library was damaged by fire (accordin to tradition, in 1609), but three of its five original bays wit their fine oak roof survive, together with three impressiv lecterns; it now acts as an occasional exhibition area.

The Wren Library

Opposite: the Chapter Hous

BUILDING AFTER 1300

Once the Angel Choir and Cloister were built, the Cathedral was substantially complete. Work in the 14th Century included insertion of the great west window and the Bishop's Eye rose window. A major addition in 1311 was the Central Tower, raised to a height of 271 feet and capped by a spire of oak and lead rising a further 200 feet. The bell, *Great Tom*, which is hung in this tower, has a long history. It is mentioned in the Chapter Acts of 1305, and has been recast several times, last in 1834. It weighs 5¼ tons and to date is the thirteenth largest in England. The Cathedral has a ring of twelve bells; the tenor weighs 23 cwt., 3 qrs., and is tuned to D. These hang in the S.W., or St. Hugh's, Tower. The Company of Ringers, founded in 1614, is the oldest in the country.

The focus of building activities in the 15th Century turned to chantry or memorial chapels, so that the Russell, Longland and Fleming Chantries adjacent to the Angel Choir were all built in the Perpendicular style. The spectacular sight of the Central Tower and its spire later included the spires on the western towers, whose belfries were raised in 1420. All three spires have gone, the central spire tower supposedly collapsing in a gale in 1549 and the western spires causing such problems of instability and weight that their dismantling in 1807 was inevitable, though wildly unpopular among the townspeople.

Every century since has seen a period of repair and changes in attitude towards the requirements of the church for worship, causing alterations in the furnishings. After the damage done during the Civil War in the 17th Century, the Cathedral was to receive some remarkable gifts; Dean Honywood's Library, the brass lectern and candelabrum in the Choir, a new wooden reredos, now under the Library stairs, and *cathedra*.

In the 18th Century there were major restorations by the architect Gibbs and, later in the century, Essex. Much of the medieval glass was also restored and reset during this century and the 17th Century reredos replaced by the present stone one.

In the 19th Century the plastered vaults in the Angel Choir and the Chapter House were 'scraped' and the choir stalls were repaired, restored and stained. Where there was evidence, some paintwork was partly restored. All the glass in the Nave is from this period and the re-leading and re-setting of older glass was part of the restoration work.

During the 1920s the interior of the west front and the four central pillars at the crossing were virtually packed with liquid cement blown through small rectangles which can still be identified in the stonework. The development of compressed air-driven jack hammers helped hasten the work and avoid too much vibration. The Ingersoll-Rand compressor is still in use in the Works Yard. A visitor to the Cathedral will, at any time, find repair work in progress somewhere in the roof or on the stone fabric. It is a continuous process.

Opposite: view of the Cloister Garden from the Wren Library. The Garden contains fragrant plants and plants associated with the Virgin Mary.

Mason examining a weathered angel on a pinnacle

Repairs in progress inside the Wren Library

THE ASSOCIATION OF THE FRIENDS OF LINCOLN CATHEDRAL

The 'Fraternity of Lincoln' was a great and important society in the middle ages to which king, queen, lords, ladies and people of all ranks and degrees belonged.

Its modern counterpart is the Association of the Friends of Lincoln Cathedral, founded in 1936 to 'bind together all those who, loving Lincoln Cathedral, are prepared to bear a part in its maintenance and adornment'.

Children between the ages of 7 and 12 can become Young Friends of the Cathedral. For those who live near enough there is one meeting in each school holiday. Those who live further away can become Associate Members.

If you feel that you would like to have a share in preserving and beautifying this great church you will be helping the Cathedral to fulfil its function as a witness to the Christian Faith and as a glorious and inspiring work of art.

Details from the Hon. Sec.: 4 Priorygate, Lincoln, LN2 1PL

CATHEDRAL GUIDES

A team of experienced guides including those who speak French, German and Norwegian is always ready to show visitors round the Cathedral. Booked parties can be catered for, including schools, the blind or disabled. Roof tours are very interesting, but a charge has to be made for these otherwise tours are free. Enquiries to the Visitor Officer.

THE CATHEDRAL SCHOOL

Lincoln School for boys goes back to the earliest years of Bishop Remigius. The School had acquired a high scholastic reputation by the middle of the 13th Century. The School has continued down to the present local comprehensive school, Lincoln Christ's Hospital School. In 1921 the old Choir School closed. The present Cathedral School was re-opened in September 1961 as a preparatory school for boys in order to educate Minster choristers. There are presently 122 boys in the school, aged between 6½ and 13. Accommodation is provided for 43 boarders, some of whom are weekly boarders.

The School is established in the Anglican tradition but pupils of all denominations and faiths attend.

Enquiries: Telephone (0522) 23769 or 28489, or write to the Headmaster, The Cathedral School, Eastgate, Lincoln LN2 1QE.

THE FABRIC FUND

What does the Fabric Fund do? The Fund is responsible for obtaining and controlling the large sums of money required to repair and restore the Cathedral. We need a great deal of money to pay our skilled workforce of stonemasons, carpenters, plumbers and glaziers; and pay for materials, tools, services, contractors, consultants and architects.

How do we find the money? With your help and also from donations, covenants, grants, legacies and loans. The Fund receives no help from Central Government Funds or the Church Commissioners, so we need your help to raise every penny required.

Enquiries to the Fabric Fund Director,
4 Priorygate,
Lincoln, LN2 1PL.

For all enquiries: (0522) 544544, or write to the Chapter Clerk, Lincoln Cathedral, LN2 1PZ.

Printed in Great Britain.
Published by English Life Publications Ltd. of Derby.
The painting on page 1 is by permission of Lincs. County Council Recreational Services: Usher Gallery, Lincoln.
Photography by Newbery Smith Associates.
Front cover colour photograph by Judges Postcards Ltd., Hastings.
Photograph of the Head Shrine is by Chris Rees.
Photograph on page 3 is by John Turner.
Plan of the Cathedral is by David Vale.
ISBN 0 85101 270 1.
© English Life Publications Ltd. 1989.

Back cover: the Judgment Porch with its exquisite carvings was the triumphal entry to the Angel Choir and its shrines.